As If Anything Can Happen

As If Anything Can Happen

Poems by

Rasma Haidri

Kelsay Books

Cover photo by Rasma Haidri copyright 2017

ISBN: 13-978-1-945752-99-5

Kelsay Books
Aldrich Press
www.kelsaybooks.com

For my mother

Acknowledgments

Grateful acknowledgment is made to the editors of the following journals and anthologies in which these poems or earlier versions of them first appeared:

Panoply: "Fish Swim the Moon"
Adanna: Women and Art: "The Lessons of Oz"
Cyclamens and Swords: "Stop and Turn"
Earth's Daughters: "Ask It" (previously published as "Us"); "Hunger" (previously published as "Palau"); "Friends and Apparitions"
Fish Stories IV: "The Last Photograph of My Father"
Ice Floe: "Miracle Maker"
The I-70 Review: "Raccoon" and "Fault"
Muzzle Magazine: "Vacancy"
Prairie Schooner: "Lottery"
Umbrella Journal: "Lesson on Perspective"
The Wallace Steven's Journal: "Omen" (previously published as "Blackbirds")

"After the Funeral" was included in *All We Can Hold* (Sage Hill Press, 2016); "Force of Circumstance" was included in *Burden of Light: Poems on Illness* (Short Fuse, 2014); "Night Clothes" under the title "My Daughter's Pajamas" was included in *Eating Her Wedding Dress* (Ragged Sky Press, 2009); "Still Brother" was commissioned as a braille inscription on a portrait by Thomas Ferrella in *Borderland*, a joint exhibit of photography and poetry for the blind, Madison, Wisconsin, 2009; "Lottery" was the subject of an essay on editing poetry in *Poem, Revised* (Marion Street Press, 2008); "Heaven" was included in *A Christmas Collection* (July Literary Press, 2001); "Still Life" (previously published as "Returning Home Late") was included in *The Pocket Parenting Guide* (Puddinghouse Press, 1999).

Contents

I.

II.

III.

About the Author

I.

Fault

I lay upside-down in the backseat,
Detroit's neon road signs flashing past.

In the front seat, parent-talk,
the word *fault,* our names.

I wondered which of us would get it,
this *fault,* this ice-cream-drink with a straw.

Suddenly I saw it on a billboard just as I
imagined: a glass of frothy vanilla fault.

Dad didn't slow the car. Mom
sucked her cigarette to liquid fire.

Their voices hissed and sputtered.
Whose *fault* would it be?

I figured my older sister would get it.
She always got things first.

Hunger

We loved Dad's *puris* best of all,
doughy flour balls he rolled in his palm, then
flattened thin with a rolling pin.

When he slid them into hot oil
the puris puffed like flying saucers.
In his boyhood Delhi, the street vendors hawked,
One rupee for puris and the pilau is free!
Acha, okay (we chorused along) ... *give me just the pilau!*

He fed them to us hot, not stopping to eat
as the puris mounted high on Mom's turkey platter.
We gobbled them, greedy, gleeful, folding the oily,
stretchy bread over saffron yellowed carrots, potatoes,
square chunks of beef, eating with our fingers as if we were
real children of India, not Detroit born and Tennessee raised.

After he died, I dreamed my father cooking.
He had only onions, and we doubted this meal,
eyeing each other in the dining room as he chatted
from the kitchen, his hands busy, the hot oil sizzling
promise, or warning.

The Lessons of Oz

Once a year, for seven years, I watched,
terrified by the tornado and snatching trees,
baffled by Dorothy walking all that way without eating,
and not once needing to use the bathroom.

Older, able to withstand the flying monkeys by repeating
it's only a movie under my breath, and imagining a film crew
and director with megaphone just off screen—
I still speculated they must have fitted her with a special pouch.

Only later did I learn how we turn off the camera, walk away,
reappear in new scenes, clicking our heels and starting over,
as if anything can happen.

Non-stop Loop

We were the same girls walking from school
as we had been walking to it,
but the sidewalk ran the wrong way.

My sister reached to ring the bell
and we waited for Mom to unlock
herself from the house.

Radio music loud, her belly big
with a baby, lipstick arching like bird wings
into a red *O* when she saw us home early.

The president died, my sister said,
stepping through the door like Joe Friday.
Mom didn't react so I added,

President Kennedy was shot,
what we were told to say.
She crumpled, turned, tugged

on the dials of her brand-new FM
stereo-console radio, playing
commercial-free non-stop

loops of music, now just a whirr
of bleeps and bloops
and static that hurt our ears.

Vacancy

Awake between them in the front seat,
guardrails flashing past, I felt her arm cross my chest
in case of impact, heard her whimper
as he barked, *Should I smash into this post?*

I watched the road for signs—not red ones flashing *No! No!*
but the liquid green *Vacancy!*—a promise
that someone waited up for us,
someone had keys for every little hook
and would call us by our names.

Not that Kind

Dalmatian in the ditch
unequivocally spot-patched,
frozen in profile
as if running,
but dead.

She didn't tell
the family where their pet was.
It wasn't that kind
of pet, not that kind
of family.

She didn't tell,
and no one
went looking for the dog.

Physics at Breakfast

He called it *dancing*, a drop of water
convulsing in wild sputters
on the wide round cast iron pan.

Before eating our omelets, Dad wanted us
to understand what happens when water
meets its match in heat.

Another swollen drop fell
from his finger—*dancing*, he said.

I saw no choreography,
only death throes, spastic twirls,
gray blobs in futile defiance
of diminishing.

What did I know of steam, evaporation,
solid-liquid-gas conversion—I thought
I was witnessing the scientific fact
of disappearance.

Each drop hung, gathering courage,
and I worried about something I had no word for,
but learned to call *oblivion*.

Still Brother

My first brother was not born
to this world.
He never looked like me, though
I would have recognized myself in his shuttered eyes
when he slipped through the wound
the surgeon made in our mother's
nine-month belly.

Once, when Mom leaned to tuck me in—black room, white bed,
Mom a gray silhouette—I saw from outside myself,
my small arms reach for her wonderful tummy.
She recoiled with a small grunt.

Then Mom and Dad vanished. A sitter came,
she took the sugar away, said we'd eat our cereal plain.
It may as well have been dirt we chewed
in that heavy world behind Mom's green drapes.

Thirty years later, Mom made the same
small grunt when I, hugely pregnant with my own
firstborn, asked if there had been
a burial, a name.

She said she had nothing to say, except
it wasn't a child,
and hospitals have ways to dispose of waste.

Pearly White

Mom offered me up like a little lamb
to the flowery ladies from the Baptist Outreach Mission
who came knocking for souls to save.

They wore beige stockings seamed up the back,
heavy shoes, square and black. Mom put a nickel
in the palm of my white glove

for the collection, and I climbed into the wide, slippery
backseat of the humpbacked sedan—some religion
was better than none.

Something to Cry About

We sit reading magazines, summer
sieves in through the screen,
as does the sound of crying, far off
wailing growing louder, in a reverse Doppler effect,
first down by the road, then in the yard,
now the house. It must be one of my brothers.

Fighting again? Dad yelps in that voice
that always hits like a slap. *Come here, both of you!*
I'll hit the other one! He smirks, chews his cheek,
pleased with his wit. *Then you'll have something to cry about!*

My youngest brother staggers in—
stiff legs, arms outstretched like a cartoon somnambulist,
but for the bawling, the runnels of blood, grazed skin,
ripped shirt, spit dripping from bruised lips.
The driver of the car didn't stop.

Mom grunts. Dad groans. They rise
to tend the wounds of their son, but no one—
not father, mother, not even the sister
says, *I'm sorry. Next time you cry I'll come.*

On the Conception of a Child

I.
Like finding the perfect word to fit the shape of the *O*
that stops us. Like God breathing waves into the waters

II.
after the word was spoken. Like the perigee dip where moon
nears an event horizon—we stood on a cemetery hill

III.
called Ohio, counting pauses between lightning
and thunder, measuring distance to empyreal fire.

IV.
A pair of headstones, blank, awaiting the chiseled
names of a mother and father, paired for God's roll call.

V.
Five months later we returned at the swell of dawn
to look for names for the child.

VI.
Five months after this Christmas afternoon, when no
grieving resounded through Ohio, the snow-robed mounds

VII.
still as angels, the evergreens black and tall as God
in the nights of children

VIII.
who are born to parents who know
when to go to them,

IX.
just the moment to turn back home,
the sun brilliant in our eyes.

Forgiving Our Fathers

At the Church of Brethren in Laguna Beach, the deacon
tells me to pray for God to solve the central problem of my life,
so I pray for the Ludi land to be sold so the bank won't foreclose
on our house. Dad hasn't paid the mortgage in months.

He doesn't like being told what to do by a bank. He'd rather
wash hands of it than pay those tugs—Mom laughs at his
Indian-syncratic English, but this is serious. I've already used
my study-abroad loan to fend off one sheriff's auction. Now
the only hope is selling Ludi, a dilapidated farm not yet lost
(by some miracle of God) to my father's gleeful dabbling in
All-American-Free-Enterprise-Personal-Bankruptcy.

The deacon says: It has been done. Problem solved.
I need not wonder when or how—but now I must forgive
my father, too. The thought is absurd—
but as his house guest I'm too polite to refuse, so I say, *Dad,
I forgive you,* over and over, until I am weeping and don't know
how to stop, or if it would be unholy to interrupt and
blow my nose, so the tears and snot drip in long ectoplasm strings
as I chant forgiveness in a rhythm stronger than faith.

Back in the deacon's million-dollar home, he introduces a woman
saying, *I helped her forgive her father, too,* and I wonder
if it's a trend—then his wife goes to bed with a migraine
because she burned the quiche, and I hear him call his daughter,
Here, Sally! Sally! Here girl! and Sally, behind beveled glass,
does not answer, just sits on the sculpted carpeting, constructing
towers from colored blocks, then toppling them over.

Ars Nostalgia

When I had been married
one year
and eight days,
I gave myself a bouquet,

then hung the gasping flowers to dry,
pressed some flat,
put them in a drawer in my desk
with all the rest

that awaits posterity—
muted petals,
recorded days,
sketches, poems, letters,

mementos, hoarded bits
of exquisiteness,
and disembodied fragments
that could be glued.

Come, you who will unearth
my archeology,
blow away the dust, watch it settle
like so much ash.

Signs

You will be born this day,
because across the road

a man with one leg
is mowing his lawn,

and the students leaving school
don't laugh at him,

or stand around smoking,
but stroll in small groups,

some of them on skateboards
listening to walkmen,

some walking backwards
to keep a conversation going,

all of them carrying small red bibles
handed out by Gideons,

old men in sky-blue suits
who pile like clowns from a tiny car

then stagger forth, arms outstretched
like toddlers offering testaments—

and the teens smile thanks,
and do not throw the books on the ground,

or at the one-legged man mowing his lawn,
but cup them in their palms,

like flames in the crowning
summer afternoon.

Restricted Deed

The crabapple dropped its petals
before I could snap the photo I planned to call:
Baby and Spring Blossom. It will not bloom again
for two years.

I am seeking some kind of beauty. Not
these green lawns that an earlier generation
groomed foursquare into retirement.
Not the war my neighbors wage with palsied arms
on dandelions.

I mind them from my window, raking, weeding,
then sitting in patio chairs, sipping coffee,
reading bad news in the papers,
now rising again to sweep and cart
away pebbles, bending and lifting in silence,
as if silence were peace, as if the world
was this street.

We move in young, bring forth children
to toddle on the lawns. Some couples settle
eagerly, boast they will retire here, cement
the legs of swing sets, add on a room
they call *rec*.

I want to live among untamed sage and ponderosa,
pressed against the thigh of a mountain—I turn
from the window, taunted by cumulus
gathered on the Wisconsin horizon, in shapes
like the Rockies.

Omen

Driving over a hill I see
        a sudden blackbird—circling overhead,
flapping wings
        flashing red—our car
speeds past
        its flattened mate—the end of love
is behind us, and I see
        my white-knuckled hand
gripping his thigh,
        not a word to spare between us.

II.

Lesson on Perspective

I stand at the far left edge
of a broken street,

a place I never wanted to be,
watching you recede

in perfect proportion to funneling gutters
and brownstone roof peaks,

your leaving unexpectedly clear,
like a page in my childhood

See-To-Draw book
I stared into, wondering

who invented the manifestation
of distance: See,

the large man is very close,
the smaller man farther away,

and the tiny man
(who may be turning his head

for one last look)
is at the vanishing point.

Raccoon

On the road in my headlight's glare
lies the body of my child—no,
a raccoon—but this *is* how she sleeps
on her side, back curled, short thighs,
feet balanced one atop the other,
all the toes at rest.

Shall I feel tender toward the raccoon,
this menace and pest? This creature,
the size of my baby daughter, may be full grown,
a mother, whose young at this moment
forage as she taught them, for food.

They will not notice her missing
until dawn, the hour raccoons
settle to sleep, the hour
I will lift my child's waking body,
whisper into her hair as she
suckles her morning milk.

Friends and Apparitions

I share the horses' sweet corn,
crack its molasses pleasure between my molars
with Star, Heather, Thunder, and the colt I found
in the field, newborn, no bigger
than a German Shepherd.

In the pasture behind Crawdad Creek
where stink flowers grow as tall as me, I wait,
still as stone, hoping that possum will come
so close I can tame her with my charm,

but she spies me and goes all petrified, so I turn away,
and that's when I see it—the air! It's everywhere,
shiny, wobbling like a see-through ripple—it's a sign,
a miracle—I know more than science,
the invisible can be seen!

Should I tell? The horses swish and snap
their tails right through it, whip-poor-wills soar, oblivious,
and polecats skit down holes as if they don't even see it
waving over us like God's laundry.

I have been chosen. The air appears
to me alone. My hands reach
for the shimmering, certain that my next gift
will be to embrace it.

As Far as I Can See

Gray highway passes under
the car, cachunk cachunk,
like a conveyor belt that will dump
us at our destination.

I ask Dad which one
of all these cars was first.
He says, Honey, they come and go,
on and off, at entrances and exits
like this one.

I say I know that.
I can see that much for myself.
I want to know which car was *first*.

He smiles, not at me,
keeps driving.

I look down the long road,
at the red-lit rear ends
of all those cars.
Someone up there knows
who's first. All I know is,
it will never be us.

The Red Balloon

My daughter brings home a red balloon, looks through it like stained glass, directing sunlight through the crimson globe, turning asphalt red, all birds to cardinals. Peering into the balloon she says, *Blood dripping, what if all the world were red, like blood dripping?*

How much blood has she known in four years? The bright scarlet line of a paper cut. The dark bulbous speck of a thumb prick. In what red dream would she wound the world?

She bicycles, the red balloon, tied to her wrist, bobbing after. Like a buoy, it marks the corner where she stops to look for cars. She unties it in the park, holding the string between her teeth, cementing it into bubble gum with her tongue.

It anchors there till something makes her speak, and the balloon lifts. She watches the red globe rise, nod and dip. She holds it with her eye, till all the red in the world fills one speck in the infinite sky.

Ignorant and Wise

Dana Ma-Lou gave Mom directions,
saying her house would be
on the "wrong" side of the road.

I worried about the circumstances
in which we'd find our new maid,
and why, if it was the wrong side,
didn't she get out of there?

All along the winding drive to Jellico
up Highway 25, I eyed the roadsides,
hoping they balanced each other out,
the good and bad, our car keeping to the middle
or a little to the right.

She called her mom *mamaw,* so I knew
she wasn't regular. Sure enough,
she looked a hundred, chewing on a corncob,
rocking flat over the weeds that poked
through porch boards around her bare old feet.

Driving home, Mom said they were *ignorant,*
not *dumb.* I had to ask what "ignorant" meant.
She said they just hadn't learned things, but that
sounded dumb to me, about as dumb as staying
on the wrong side when everyone knew the other was right.

The Clergyman's Daughter

Here, Father, is your saint,
twisted and gnarled like a northern birch.

A lifeline slices each of my palms,
but they don't match. I dared not ask

if the women singing in angel-tongue
rehearsed.

All lacey curls and confusion, a bride
of Christ, I pierced my thigh

with a hatpin and began
to understand God.

Father, you lied that a clergyman's daughter
would give birth to soldiers.

My child waited ten days, Father,
for the stars to align before being born.

Who dares to name
the hour God breathed in her soul?

She tells me she climbs a ladder, Father,
to bathe in the dust of stars.

She says she came from the stars, Father.
She will scatter them over my scars.

Naming It

Though I hear it is him in the background, I ask
who, when you say *we think.*

I remember pink tiles in the foyer where I lay,
my big belly holding you,

my pink plaid maternity top
and matching pants,

spit on my cheek where he leaned
close, shaking me to my senses

for the nothing I did, the something
I didn't —maybe I didn't say *we* think…

I think I was trying to think
when he forced me down, pinned my arms

the way, he said, men sometimes had to do.
Floating inside me, you heard his hiss

and shout, felt the knot, the strangled sinew
of my voice, struck dumb-numb-mute—

I couldn't name this then—no
words mean how it is

to live comatose, smile pulled tight,
posing for the yearly portrait.

It took me a lifetime to leave. You love him and I don't
want you not to—but wonder,

as I grip the phone, if you still feel
the knot tighten inside me,

when in your voice
I hear his words.

Beggared

He said people
give beggars
money to make
themselves
feel good,

so it's selfish
to give money
to gypsies just to
keep yourself
from feeling bad.

A generation
of beggars
came and went
before I thought:

why not
do something
to make
myself feel good?

Ask It

One day when I visit, my mother
is missing a tooth. When she speaks, one side

of her lip caves in, I see her sagging cheeks,
a fold of skin waving uselessly

below her chin, and she looks like old women
looked when I was seven—I can't

look at her, nor look away, nor ask the question
as my daughter bounces past us,

ponytail flashing, showing off
her one-legged hop.

Aubade

I tiptoe past her room, hear that she
awakened, too, is reaching for a book.

At my writing desk, I stop mining for what
I thought I had to say, listen

as she turns a page, her hum-yawns
and small soprano squeaks: *Have you seen my duckling?*

words learned by heart when I read her favorite book,
the one about the mother duck

with all her babies in a row, but one.
She queries a different creature on every page,

Have you seen my duckling?
No maternal loss in my daughter's voice.

She never fears for the child, has shown me,
peering close to the page, what I didn't see:

the baby duck is always near, exploring rocks and bushes.
This is what kids do, she says,

then tells me about the unbreakable wire
that links our shoulder blades—

it is short when we are near,
and stretches to infinity.

Lost Tooth

Midnight Goddess of Milktooth
descends from the half-slice of moon
that illuminates my daughter, asleep,
her tongue already probing her new
geography.

Even now, the cells in her
iron-tasting breach are dividing,
growing new bone, rock bone,
bone that will outlive me.

Force of Circumstance

Mom crossed out entire passages of love letters,
cut away inscriptions in books, preferring scars
to her exposed intimacy.
At seventy, she confides over the phone, *it wasn't worth it,*
and I know she thinks I'm dying.

My ninth day in the hospital. She says she called
the surgeon at his house, told him he better figure
something out to stop the bleeding in my kidneys.
Then she tells me about Detroit, how she stayed up nights,
furiously scribbling poems and eating puffed rice,
while our bottles boiled.

I remember the electric blue Smith Corona
Dad bought for her poems. I was the one who used it,
triggering the carriage return like a gun,
practicing the backward-upside-down paper insertion,
trilling my fingers over the keys until they stuck mid-air
in combinations I wrote down as code.

She preferred scrawling her loopy lines
on Dad's defunct business letterhead,
her scraps of verse and hand-stapled revisions
got moved from house to house
in a cardboard box.

She says of the excised words, *I've thought about it
the past fifteen years or so, and realize they were only for me.*
Then she adds, *I could still crank out a few poems,*
as if bargaining for my life, or her own.

Miracle Maker

I rode bareback,
no bridle, no hands,
told the horse
with my strong
thinking where to go
and she did—

or I kept changing my mind
as she grazed
between patches of clover.

The possum
I thought I'd tamed
with my powers
when it followed
from the woods
to our house

was shot dead
by the sheriff who was called
by my mother
who was called
by me
to come and see the miracle.

Probably rabid,
the sheriff said
and I
began to doubt God.

III.

Diagnostic Investigation

The X-ray shows two strings
dangling from kites
the doctor says are my kidneys.

He examines a tiny frazzle on one string
as I watch the kites sparring—cloud dragons
on hind legs, forepaws raised for boxing
like the flaming white dragons
on my daughter's Chinese fans.

When I return from the hospital,
she dances for me, a fan in each hand,
her small body twirling, bending, making the fans twist,
then fall, then rise,
the dragons swaying over our heads.
Her eyes never leave my face.

Night Clothes

I dream the neighbor girl and her father
night-prowl our yard,
looking for Barbie's bathrobe,
Black and white fur! they call,
the girl gripping the doll's hard breasts
through thin pajamas,
the father's hands thrust in his pockets.

*We don't understand
how we lost it,* they cry,
creeping through the trees
that darken the house.

My daughter appears
behind me on the porch,
still damp from her shower,
her wet hair a mass of gold tangles,
her narrow hairless body,
round breast buds exposed,
as she dries her back with a towel.

She shouts, *We'll find it, don't worry!*
and goes on drying herself,
unaware and unashamed of her naked body,
which is all she has ever slept in.

Fish Swim the Moon

The moon rises orange,
cords of black cloud circling
her pregnant belly.

My daughter drew Jupiter
this way, using thirty-seven
shades of red, tracing each ring
one atop the other, placing each
yellow moon in orbit.

The teacher wrote *Late!*
at the top of the page.

Nothing is ever late.

Not this carillon tolling.
Not this wind tossing litter.
Not this Jupiter rising over black water
where a fish swims the moon
and we walk without drowning.

Lottery

Everything my mother needs can be found
at Woodman's: cigarettes, milk, unsalted rice cakes,
six black bottles of diet cola.

I want to buy a lottery ticket, she adds,
weaving stiff-kneed, half-blind, to the far end
of the store, near videos and packaged liquor.

Neither of us knows how to go about it.
I fumble, rubbing in the dots from numbers
she has scribbled on a scrap of cardboard.
I look at her familiar cursive,
wondering what they are—not our ages, birthdays,
not her wedding anniversary.

That's six and a half million a year for life,
she says of the man who won last winter,
and I don't ask how she figured the years left in his life.

Nor do I ask if the money could buy back
her teeth and eyes, her strong bones and lean flesh,
buy back the summers she played squirt guns with us
and caught fireflies we froze and sold to science
for thirty cents a hundred.

No one has claimed it, she whispers,
as if everything is still possible.

Heaven

Each Christmas Eve we made pilgrimage
to your wood plank Polish church.
The fir tree's starry lights eclipsed the altar
and the cross of Christ, but all I knew or needed of holy
was in your solo.

Your young round face, hair like thistle,
was barely visible beyond the ranks of farmers
who hushed at your song, as if Gabriel had come.

All the way home, I lay in the bumpy back of our
station wagon, drunk with your refrains,
watching star windows,
each an angel-filled porthole in the night web,
the dark matter of God.

When you were twenty-one, a phone call came
on an afternoon so glorious nothing could be wrong.
You chuckled about your skin,
a shade of green the doctors couldn't explain.
At the hospital, they wouldn't let me bring my baby in.

Seven days later you died, as if you knew just how to
go about it—plunge into heaven— while we
were still learning to pronounce your disease
and get the spelling.

A nurse thrusts your trousers into my hands
saying, *Remove the money*. They are tailored black worsted,
so like you, always spiffy, rather formal, dressed for a funeral.
I drop the coins beside your untouched glass of water.

Outside, the air sticks in my throat,
the night stings my cheek. Heaven is a vast
confusion of dust and gasses and rock.
No angels in the windowless canopy.
Gary, are you singing?

The Last Photograph of My Father

My daughter is in his lap
like a bouquet of flowers,
like the bouquet that will come from a friend
three days later,
but that is not the miracle.

The miracle is my mother
behind his chair.
No one asked her to stand there.
Not because she didn't belong,
but my mother refuses to be in pictures,
turns her head, covers her face, scowls.
Even a wedding snapshot shows her waving
an angry arm at the photographer,
in a childhood photo she hits her kid brother
with the camera.
No one asks to take my mother's photo.

This was to be of my father and daughter,
but she got up unbidden,
crossed the room,
positioned herself behind him,
and though unpracticed, she smiled,
wanting to be there, as if she heard
his heart counting down.

Still Life

You return home late
to bright girl clutter: hairbrushes, ribbons,
balled up socks and glitter.

Do not touch a thing.
There is nothing to put away;
no such place as *away* to put things.

How perfectly your daughters
have left evidence of their abundance.
Leave it. Go to them.

This is the beginning of the painting
in which they will show you
who you are.

Caught off Guard

Typical of Mom, she's padlocked her bedroom door
from the inside. I remember the ice pick she held, poised
and ready, in our New York apartment elevator,
and how she made me, age seven, stand guard by public
men's rooms *in case of perverts,* to protect my little brothers.

We phoned all morning, then drove over,
now we've been knocking on the bedroom door for hours.
We knock, call, then retreat into the condo's
open living area, as if luring her to join us.

When we got here the blinds were down, a thing she hates,
What will the neighbors think?
Yesterday she said, *You have beautiful eyes.*
Of course you never do anything with them.
This morning, for the first time, I wore mascara.
This morning, for the first time, she didn't draw the shades.

Now hope is a caul my voice would break—
now the pounding would wake the dead.
I collect the children like chicks—*don't move,*
don't go near—as my husband bashes the door—it gives,
he falls in, reels back out nodding, Yup, she's dead.
How do you know? I cry, hand off the children,
cross the splintered frame.

She sits on the edge of her daybed, feet planted,
a palm on each thigh, her eyes blue and surprised, leaning
slightly back as if about to laugh—and in the bedroom a child
is calling, *my mommy!* as I stare at the wide blue scar down her
belly, where my brothers emerged like small emperors.
My mommy! She doesn't answer, this stranger in my mother's
body, wearing what my mother never wore, and certainly never
would be caught dead in: a bra and pink bikini underwear.

After the Funeral

The moon, dumb
      as a stone in winter,
pulls like a tide,
      makes me look up
when I want to look away,
      makes me stop
when I want to breathe
      my own breath again,
tuck my soul back in—
      it startles
like a naked breast,
      pearly as a porcelain doorknob
in my mother's house,
      where the blinds
stayed shut.
      Now the empyrean drapes
fling open,
      exposing me
to the moon's
      glaring interrogation:
Where did she go?
      I wonder if she hunkers
on the shadow side —
      Mom, the moon
haunts and taunts
      me—Mom,
the moon is cruel to me—Mom?
      The sky
has never been this empty.

Shopping at K-Mart for My Dead Mother

Cartons of Carlton 100s at the checkout
make me stop, whirl the cart back to Candy & Snacks—
my daughter squealing with glee as I snatch
Snackwells Fat Free Devil's Food Cakes,
Peppermint Patties in their happy foil, a red plaid box
of Genuine Lorna Doone Shortbread.

Nanny would have bought you these, I say,
grabbing Kit Kats, Chicken-in-a-Biscuit, Original Low-Fat
Fig Newtons, and look—here are the size XXX
men's black sweatshirts I'm always supposed to buy,
but never find, or forget, so she says, *You don't try.*

Now look at me—three days after the funeral,
and it's never been so easy—
reeling through aisles, the cart holding only our jackets,
and beginner bras for my daughter,
which is what we came for.

All the Comforts of Home at Holiday Inn

We always arrived after dark,
Mom needing coffee
and nothing open but the ice machine.

Dad ran scalding tap water
into a glass of instant crystals, stirred
with a ballpoint pen.

Sometimes he plugged a metal coil into the wall,
then submerged it in a cup of water.
This would've electrocuted me, but for him
the water boiled, and Mom got her coffee.

At every restaurant I ordered fried shrimp.
Waited, bored, for others to decide, as if there
were any reason to eat anything else
if you could eat shrimp.

Once I sulked and cried myself to sleep
in the white porcelain bathtub,
to make a point,
but no one came to get me out.

We were allowed to jump on beds,
twisting, squealing, holding our breath,
and when we lay down,
Dad slipped a quarter into a slot
to make the bed jiggle and shake.

Today, the hotel bed is bolted to the floor,
no quarter slot for a massage, no bathtub
to lie down in to sleep, or cry.

Just Mr. Coffee in the bathroom,
paper packets of caffeine powder,
fake sugar, fake cream,
plastic stir sticks—and both my parents
long buried under a red stone.

Stop and Turn

I sort through the bank box for our marriage certificate,
signed by Terri, Always-A-Bridesmaid-Never-A-Bride,
and Darrell, my Ex-Boyfriend-At-The-Time, who warned you:
She'll demand too much. Neither of us knew what he meant.
There wasn't a pair of twenty-one-year-olds
as in love as we were in 1979.

I rub the carbon smudges from my fingers, hoping the bleary
document will pass the commissioner's authenticity test, then see
the tiny print: *Copy for the bride and groom.*
They thought we'd only need one.

Later, I watch our fourteen-year old daughter pack her bag
for *two weeks at Papa's.* I see her to your car, speak through the
window to your profile, *Here are the forms I got...* a scraggly
gray beard where I recall the thick brown moustache
you didn't shave till age thirty.

I hand you the documents decreeing our divorce, a stamped
envelope pre-addressed to the commissioner's office, assuming
the business tone that long ago became our mode of
communication. We're still good at it, for the sake
of the children, or ourselves.

For my sake, I've taken up what you always called *a waste*—
photographing windows and doors, bits of weathered wood,
broken panes, twisted iron, any bit of beauty or curiosity
that makes me stop and turn my head. Lately, it's been
storefront mannequins.

Imagine my luck—one night in Trondheim, I found a
pair of ivory nudes, a man and woman, statuesque from

the neck down, headless on top. I shot them where they stood,
ripe and poised, confident, as if they already wore beautiful
clothes, as if they were someplace else—not engulfed in
oblivion, waiting to be snapped, framed, hung on my wall,
a portrait I named: *Now Try to Kiss the Bride.*

About the Author

Rasma Haidri grew up in Tennessee and makes her home on the arctic seacoast of Norway. Her poems and essays appear widely in anthologies, literary journals, and college textbooks in the USA and abroad. Literary distinctions for her writing include the Southern Women Writers Association Emerging Writer Award in creative non-fiction, the Wisconsin Academy of Arts, Letters & Science poetry award, the Easy Street Great American Sentence prize, and a Best of the Net nomination. Read more of her work at www.rasma.org

www.ingramcontent.com/pod-product-compliance
Lightning Source LLC
LaVergne TN
LVHW021623080426
835510LV00019B/2739